The Angel Inside

The Angel Inside

*Inspiration to
Connect With Your
Inner Guidance*

Ashley A. Barnes, MS

True Bliss Publishing
Louisville, Kentucky

Copyright © by Ashley A. Barnes, MS

All rights reserved.
Published in the United States of America
by True Bliss Publishing
of Louisville, Kentucky
www.aspiritledlife.org

Barnes, Ashley A.

The Angel Inside

Without limiting the rights under copyright reserved previously, no part of this publication, other than for short reviews by journalist, may be reproduced, stored in or introduced into a retrieval system, or transmitted, in any form, or by any means (electronic, mechanical, photocopying, recording, or otherwise), without the prior written permission of the copyright owner.

While the author has made every effort to provide accurate contact information at the time of publication, neither the publisher nor the author assumes any responsibility for errors, or for changes that occur after publication. Further, the publisher does not have any control over and does not assume any responsibility for author or third-party Web sites or their content.

ISBN- 13: 978-0-6927-1999-2
ISBN- 10: 0692719997

Printed in the United States of America

True Bliss Publishing
Louisville, KY

True Bliss Publishing release date May 2016

Dedication

In honor of my mother:
without her spirit and tenacity,
this book would not exist.

And for my husband, Jake,
my rock and my biggest supporter.

And for all the angels in my life,
both seen and unseen.

Contents

Foreword..x
Preface...xiii
How to Use this Guide...xvii
Introduction..1

Part 1: Meet Your Angel Inside   3

Humans as Spiritual Beings.......................................4
Connection, Our Gift of Love...................................10
Hearing the Voice Inside..14

Part 2: Benefits of Connecting   21

Peace that Passes Understanding............................22
Divine Love...26
Simple Focus...30
Balance Within..34
Spiritual Abundance..40
Healing from Within..44
True Purpose..48
Nourishing Relationships..54
Co-Creation with Spirit...58
Minimized Suffering..62
Transition to Wholeness..68

Part 3: How to Connect — 75

Retreat Inward..76
Silence the Mind..82
Practice Gratitude..88
Let Go..94
Support Well-being..100
Move Mindfully..106
Engage in Creative Expression....................................110
Experience Nature..114
Explore the Senses..120
Cultivate Love...126

Part 4: The Journey Forward — 131

The Time is Near...132
The World is Changing...136
Waking Up...140
Heaven on Earth..146
The Start of Something New 152

Afterword...156
Final Reflections...158
Acknowledgments...163
About The Author...167

Editor:
    Sara Loy / Savvy Communication, LLC
Cover Design:
    Transcendent Publishing
Interior Layout Design:
    Sybil Watts / NewSoft Publishing

We invite you to look deeper inside
where silence overrides the noise
where the gentle whisper overrides the silence.
That is your soul.
Go deeper, leave this world behind.
Find us. We are here and we love you.

Foreword

The vast technological advances of the past century have taught us to rely mostly on what we can measure with instruments or see, taste, touch smell or feel. Society has taught us to trust things outside ourselves, which has caused us to tune out our connection to our Source. The unfortunate consequence is that we have stopped trusting our own intuition, which has kept us from our full potential and happiness.

Despite the improvements made in the western world in areas of health, technology and social media, many people experience feelings of disillusionment, loneliness, even despair. No amount of material wealth, food, relationships, or distractions can fill the void. We have found many ways to avoid going within to find what our own inner voice is trying to tell us—the important messages that can help us find true peace and fulfillment. Something seems to be missing, yet so many seem clueless as to how to find answers.

I understand how easily we can be pulled off our own center by following anything or anyone that keeps us from having to look within for our own answers. However, I have also learned that God has not left us alone, without any help. Rather, he/she devised an ingenious plan to help us by providing continuous expert assistance through angels.

Growing up, while attending weekly church services, I learned a little bit about angels. Although I felt many angels with me, I still did not know how to actively communicate with them for my highest good. I was not taught how to do that.

However, as I grew older, I began to meditate, and through the process of meditation and prayer, I began to have a more intimate and fulfilling relationship with the angels that God sent to assist me on my life's journey. I have encountered many angels, some who appeared in physical form, and many who show their presence to me in other ways.

After publishing my book, *Harmony and Me*, (Chicago Spectrum Press) a book about my personal meeting with Angel Harmony, I dedicated my life to empowering people by helping them believe in a loving Creator who sends angels to help us and who wants us to learn how to trust our own inner wisdom and guidance.

Since 2006, alongside my husband, composer Michael Fess, Spirit has worked through us to help people find their own connection to their Source, while learning how to meet and develop a relationship with their own angels and spiritual guides. Through our keynote speaking, musical performances, writings, classes, individual sessions, and guided meditations we have empowered many thousands of individuals. Most people we meet want to know more about their angels.

If you want to meet your own angels and develop a relationship with them, then you will truly benefit from *The Angel Inside*. Ashley Barnes is blessed with integrity, compassion, faith, and the rare ability to communicate what she knows and has experienced for the benefit of people in all walks of life. She is able to share with us specific ways that you can communicate with your angels. In fact, she has developed a guide to help you do just that. I wish I had this guide when I was beginning my own spiritual journey.

Reading *The Angel Inside*, leads to a change in our perception of reality and our understanding of what it really means to enjoy the wonderful communion with angels on an every day basis as they gently guide us to greater heights of self-love, peace, self-empowerment and spiritual growth.

In the same way that technological advancements and social media have broadened our horizons, so too, *The Angel Inside* helps reclaim our ability to trust in the unseen, to believe in miracles, to relax, knowing we are always carefully guided by angels who are here to assist in the ascension of humankind.

Cindy Fess
January 13, 2016

Preface

This book was divinely guided. Demanded, to be more accurate. I've come to learn in recent years that Divine guidance has a way of doing that, especially if you don't act when you're instructed to do so. You see, I've known for some time that I have a deep longing in my soul to do something greater in life, that a larger purpose has been calling me, nagging me to break out of my mold and do something different. I've known since a young age that I'm meant to be of service to people in some way.

And yet, if you had asked me a few years ago, I would've told you that I didn't believe in a spiritual life path or purpose, that free will alone guides our choices in relationships, careers, hobbies, etc. I didn't believe in soul mates or spiritual beings that interact with humans to guide and assist us in our human experience. However, through a variety of experiences, I've come to realize all of that is true, and more. And it is through these experiences that I was guided to write this book.

To be clear, I didn't receive guidance directly, at least not at first. I have a very strong will and I'm very good at overriding that voice inside when I can't see the logic, the outcome, or most often, when I'm fearful. Remember the Bible story of Jonah? Jonah received direct orders from God to go to Nineveh, yet he was fearful and couldn't understand why God wanted him to go. So rather than having faith in the Divine plan, he tried to hide from God.

I suspect that attempts were made to contact me directly; however, my will is so strong, I instead received helpers in my life, people who were more open to listening and who became conduits for the message that I was too stubborn to receive. "You need to write a book. There are people who need your help and writing a book is how you need to reach them," they told me. Really, me? Write a book? I hardly had the credentials, life experience, or wisdom to write a book. What would it be about anyway? "You need to tell them about us." I stubbornly and repeatedly pushed away the idea. That was just plain scary.

Again, I reasoned, what qualifies me to write a book? My background is as varied as fish in the sea. I've worked with kids, recruited contract employees, planned corporate events, written grants, coordinated volunteers, facilitated corporate employee orientations, and managed leadership training programs. I'm a certified Integrative Nutrition Coach who doesn't actually practice. I've been divorced and remarried. My time management skills could definitely use improvement. I can lose my temper with my kids, I don't compliment my husband enough, and my diet often isn't compatible with a health coach lifestyle. The reasons why I could not– should not– write a book are endless. In short, what qualifies me to write a book that would help anyone?

And where did questioning God's plan get Jonah? In the belly of a whale, which is exactly where I found myself, hiding from the Divine, thinking that if I ignored the request, it would go away.

Nevertheless, Divine guidance did not waver. "You are enough," I heard. This guidance I received directly, and it was the exact wording I used on my original website to encourage other women to start taking care of themselves. "You are enough, you are enough, you are enough. Your life doesn't need to be exceptional to inspire someone else. We will help you."

And in the end, Jonah, too, went to Nineveh as requested.

Following My Own Guidance

This book is not the entirety of my Divine life purpose; that is yet to be revealed. However, I know beyond any shadow of a doubt that it's part of the plan. It's one step of many in my purpose to be of service. Moreover, I know that as we live our lives with free will, a gift of the Divine, there are some things that are negotiable and some that are not. Human will has the ability to override intuition; however, depending on the importance of the task to the greater world, the Divine may not make it easy to ignore the voice inside. The effects of ignoring that still, small voice– the one that knows why you exist in this world and what gifts you have to share– may be great and may take an enormous toll on you and those around you.

This book, then, is my submission to the Divine. It is me finally following my own inner voice. It is me allowing Spirit to co-create through me to bring the message of love and guidance to the world from the Angels and the Divine. My hope is that you'll find at least one nugget of inspiration for your own life and that you will be empowered to go within to find your own Angel Inside, to be courageous and follow her guidance with faith and love.

How to Use this Guide

The Angel Inside is a practical guide for daily or weekly use. Each reading includes an inspirational poem, inspired writing, and an opportunity to reflect. The reflection questions invite you to ponder the writings further. Blank lines allow you to write your thoughts and feelings on the questions. Use the space in any way that works best for you.

Throughout this guide, I use the terms "Creator," "Source," and "Divine" nearly interchangeably. With the exception of the Foreword and the Preface, I purposefully avoid using religion-specific terms such as "God". The intent is not to create or push a specific doctrine or dogma, rather, it is in the spirit of inclusiveness. My deepest hope is that the information shared here will resonate with people from all faith traditions, backgrounds, cultures, and beliefs. As you read the daily sections, if it is more comfortable to use your own language in place of these words, I encourage you to honor what is right for you.

Similarly, some parts may not resonate with you at all. In this case, I suggest you simply take what works for you at this point in your life and leave the rest here in these pages. At some point, you may return to this book and find new meaning in words or phrases that did not resonate previously. Or you may not. Either way, I have faith that you will take from this what your angels want or need you to know at this time.

With Love and Light,

Ashley Barnes

Introduction

*We invite you to look deeper inside,
where silence overrides the noise,
where a gentle whisper overrides the silence.
That is your soul.
Go deeper. Leave this world behind.
Find us. We are here and we love you.*

Who invites us to go deeper within? Who is it that whispers to our soul? They are our angels, our guides, our heavenly assistants. Our angels are messengers, helpers, tasked with guiding us through our human lives. They are loving and want only the highest good for all beings. They are a gift from the Creator, the Source of all existence, to enhance our faith, give us hope, ease our suffering, and remind us that we are not lost or alone, even in our darkest moments. They are the voice of the Divine, translated through love to us.

The angels asked for this book in order to make us aware of the many advantages of accepting their existence and opening ourselves to their constant love and guidance. The stakes are high for our own sense of peace and abundance, the manifestation of what we need and want, and for realizing our path in this life. The stakes are high

Introduction

for the world as well. Connection has a higher purpose for all beings, not only us as individuals. As we begin to accept and understand our spiritual nature, we come to understand our connection to the Creator as well as to all beings. This is our angels' goal. This is our purpose.

Part 1: Meet Your Angel Inside

Humans as Spiritual Beings

The door is open for me and you
To uncover eternity and love incarnate,
Though the keyhole remains hidden
To those who shield themselves from love
So quiet your mind, like an infant,
Languish in the pleasure of being pure
And at one with infinite life

For it was out of blackness
That the grand palm opened
Extended outward in all directions,
And life was formed

Like a great sun, a glowing ball of fire and light,
Each ray a perfect
and divine expansion of the original,
Distinct yet connected,
each extolling the Source
With its very existence

Extending into all space and time,
Drawing from the ethereal energy source
To bring light into the world,

For on the first day, out of blackness,
God created light, and it was us
And it was perfect

Since the dawning of time, spirit has been in existence. The Creator is spirit. We are spirit, and so are the angels. It is critical that we wake up to our true nature as divine beings connected to a divine Creator— *divine* as in spiritual, having a soul, existing within the body in spirit form. Inside us, we are pure and perfect spirit, like the Creator. We are made of the Creator's pure and perfect light.

Angels do not take the place of the Creator; rather they are a means of reaching the Creator when we experience disconnection while in a human body. Humanity, and especially the chattering mind, blocks out the true essence of the Creator and often our true essence as well. We experience ourselves as human, not as the spirit, or soul, within. Because they are not in human form, our angels are closer to creation energy; there is no barrier for them. Their job, then, is to help us as we experience the barrier. Connecting to them allows us to keep in touch with our soul self, the part of us that is pure energy, love, and light, the part that connects easily to the Creator and even other beings, without the barrier of being in a human body. When we reach out to our angels, they translate the Creator's love for us into guidance and caring through their connection.

Our spirits know their true home, their true origins. They know their true connection to the Source and to the angels. We only have to awaken to this knowledge and accept this reality. At our deepest core, we are them, and they are us. Imagine the Source as a great, shining sun. The Source is the ball of light in the center, and we are all the rays, each projecting in different directions, yet still part of the whole. When in a human form, we look and feel separate. However, we are never separate at the spirit level. That is where connection arises.

Reflection

Connection with our angels involves exploring the concept that we are not separate, physically or energetically. How does this open your understanding of connection?

_____

_____

_____

_____

Do you feel less alone with this understanding of connection?

_____

_____

_____

_____

Connection, Our Gift of Love

If you go where you are led
The angel inside will follow
Never leaving your side
Never leaving you alone

For the angel inside is of you
And she is outside you
Her guidance is gentle truth
In a sea of choices
Her truth is the wisdom of ages
Passed down to you in a moment
Comforting and invigorating at once

Yet you must open to her presence
You must accept her love
Her arms remain widespread
Her heart always open
For you, her love
Her angel inside

It is our angels' greatest honor to love and protect us throughout our life while we are physically disconnected from the Creator in our human bodies. Our angels still remember at the soul level what the Creator's love feels like. And they can share that with us, give us a little remembrance of heaven on earth. For, while we are on our journey, we do not have to be lost, wandering, sick. We have each a resource, a guide, a counsel, if we choose to seek them.

Like the Source, our angels are always here, and we must reach out to them. Our highest good is always their utmost concern. In all things, they bring great love to us and only want to see us happy and thriving. Yes, there will be trials and they cannot stop these from happening. However, they are with us and can help us through it, help us find inner joy and peace, even amidst great turmoil. They are here in all situations, all life events and transitions, always available to assist us. They want us to live a peaceful and happy life, fulfilled in our choices.

We can, of course, choose not to connect with our angels, yet the time has come in humanity when their existence can no longer be denied. It is important to human survival that as many as possible come to know them, come to understand our own divinity and spiritual nature, and come to experience the Creator in a different way. It is time to cast off the hate, suffering, and pain that results from feeling disconnected.

We are always surrounded by our angelic guides and helpers, and therefore, we are surrounded by the Creator. The Creator has given us this gift, to be protected and supported while we experience this life. We are the endless expression of the Creator's love. And it is for this reason that our angels' connection is available to us. Because we are loved and we *are* Love.

Reflection

Do you feel disconnected from Source? When do you experience that most?

_____

_____

_____

_____

How do you feel about the idea that you are love incarnate?

_____

_____

_____

_____

Hearing the Voice Inside

*Get out of your own mind,
fraught with worry and doubt,*

*think with your soul,
drop down into your heart,*

*open wide to reconnect
with the ancient wisdom*

*only to be found in silence,
listening with invisible ears*

*which hear deeper, wider,
more passionately than any human sense,*

*perceiving from the very depths of being,
casting out all that isn't real,*

*focusing only on that which
can be defined as love,*

*real love that causes no pain
nor cracks under pressure,*

*nor breaks when the agony of the world
becomes too much to bear,*

*real love that flows smoothly
without bumps or turns,*

*flowing with the urgency
of unconditional connection*

*to the greater Love,
the one who is love and shares love*

*outside the mind
beyond the body
in the heart of all that is*

Look at the living creatures around us. See how simply they connect to their Source. It's because they have no pretense, no expectations, no rules. Yet we have so many distractions, so many other voices that dissuade us from our true selves. Why do we listen to those other voices, when the voice inside loves us unconditionally? No, not the voices inside our heads that constantly tell us we're not enough. Those voices are a reflection of the outer world. The voice of unconditional love resides within, beneath all the worldly preoccupations. That is the voice which we are charged to find.

We call this a gift, this ability to receive our angels' messages and connect with Source. However, any of us can have this connection, if we choose, and the angels long for that. Many of us simply do not use it or even understand that it is accessible. Our traditions may tell us that it is bad. In reality, it is a loving gift from our Creator that we may stay connected while we are gone from home; we can be far away yet still connected.

There are many ways to receive our angels' messages. Their voices are subtle yet strong and only helpful if we ask and pay attention to the response, which may not always come in a clear and coherent message. The translation between spirit and human language is not always precise and each of us "hears" in different ways. We must be patient with ourselves and with them as we learn together how best to communicate.

Through all our trials and tribulations on Earth, the voice of our souls– the voice of the Creator– is with us, guiding us, loving us, if we will allow it. Each person is so very special and needed. Our angels want us to live up to our full potential. We can't let the voice of our minds override the voice of our souls anymore.

Reflection

How have you heard the voice of your angel inside? In what ways do you receive messages?

_____

_____

_____

_____

Are you willing to commit to get out of your mind and into your soul or heart in order to enhance connection?

_____

_____

_____

_____

Part 2: Benefits of Connecting

Peace that Passes Understanding

*In the deepest parts
Of the silent night of the soul
Your spirit knows,
And in the knowing, that silence,
There is a freedom of the deepest sort,
Freedom that none can touch
Or force you to surrender.*

*In that knowing, that silence,
There is a peace
That no amount of back-breaking
Or heart-shattering
Can penetrate.*

*In that space you are wholly you,
The very essence of your eternal being,
And in that space
You know.
No doubt, no fear,
Only pure knowing,
A free and peaceful soul.*

Benefits of Connecting

Peace is a gift. It is our natural state. When we cloud our minds, how do we get ourselves out of it? It could be sickness, bad diet, stress, grief, or all of these things. We can come to our angels in silence and let their ethereal embrace soothe us. Though they hold us with spiritual arms, sometimes we can even feel them wrapped around us in love and warm memories of our lives as spiritual beings.

Our spirit inside needs nourishment, the same as our bodies. Our religions attempt to provide this, yet it is primarily external. While listening to the words of another man can be inspiring and uplifting, feeling the arms of the Source wrapped around us as we sit quietly with gentle and reassuring words from our own soul– that is reaching heaven. The peace and love for which we long are not as far away as they seem. They are all around us and inside us.

It is time for us to listen, to set aside our fears and our teachings that contradict this ability, and reach out in the darkness of our minds for the light. Our angels are here. They are always here, if only we call on them. We can't wait for the neon sign or the white feather to drop from the sky. We must take action because we desire connection to our Source, to the Divine one who gives us life. The longer we wait, the more suffering the world and we endure.

This is not to say we should go against our path or ignore our free will. The angels will be with us no matter what. And the more people that find this connection, the more the world advances into an era of peace. This does not necessarily mean an end to all wars and fighting. Instead, it is an internal peace, where many beings know the love of the Creator and therefore find "the peace that passes understanding." This state of being of which Jesus spoke is real and possible right now.

Reflection

Have you considered before that peace is your natural state of being? If this is true, how might that change your outlook on life?

_____
_____
_____
_____

Are you willing to open yourself to the possibility that connection with your angels can bring you the peace you desire?

_____
_____
_____
_____

Divine Love

When words elude you
Go inside
Find that space
Where love writes the lyrics
Where the breath hums the melody
The soothing, healing melody
Of the soul

Go inside,
Find the place where you reside,
Where serenity is sacred
And your wisdom is revered,
Where all hurts are understood
And the dear one cradles you in her arms
Whenever you need a place to rest

Go inside,
Find your heart's desires
All there
All wrapped in love
All for you,
Inside

It is the great fallacy of human nature that we must look far and wide, or within four walls on a certain day, to find truth. We all seek it and we all carry it. Imagine if we connected openly with our angels and with each other, if we listened without judgment or disdain to the truths shared with us. The keys to happiness and eternal life are all around, and yet we wander and search for whole lifetimes.

Truth seems like it should be absolute and yet it isn't. The only absolute truth is Love. Not the love of humans, conditional and judgmental. The love of the Creator. For there is no greater way to love than to bring something into being, which is what the Creator did for us. Therefore, love is the only truth, that which all life is built around, and yet we humans have strayed so far. We fight for invisible truths, carried down for generations. We kill for truths that never existed except in books and traditions when all we must do is be love, share love, and grow love.

We must find the love in our souls– everyone has it – by connecting with our angels. They will show us the unconditional soul love of the Creator that we can share with others. They know this may be a difficult concept to understand. This may be unlike anything we've ever experienced. And it comes from within. We may think it is impossible to experience love like this. It is not. This is who we are. Not flesh and blood, not a thinking mind, but love. Love from the most divine Source, the originator of all life. This is who we are in our deepest, darkest moments, when our world seems bleak. We are love, pure and holy.

Reflection

How do you feel about the concept that love is the only truth?

_____

_____

_____

_____

How might it change your life if you start to see yourself as pure, unconditional love from the Source?

_____

_____

_____

_____

Simple Focus

Dear ones,
The world was made for you,
For you to experience the joys
And pain of being human,
And though you fight
Against the beingness of you
Though you deny the essence
Of your true nature
You are still loved.

A host of angels
Could not proclaim loudly enough
How much you are loved and needed
In this life.

Open your soul to the great song,
Let it blend with your bones
And course through your veins,
For you wrote it,
Your song,
An eternity ago
And it still lives in you.

It's the simplest little things that should be our focus in this life. We live with so much complexity, and yet with our angels, life could be so much simpler. Not easy, just simpler. With a daily connection, they can help guide our way, provide us solace, and fill us with peace. We can see that we don't need all the other complicated parts of life anymore. We will naturally strive for simple.

Simplicity paves the way for a more direct path and helps us to weed out those people and situations that do not serve our highest good. When we do this, our souls feel freer and not so confined by our human bodies. Then we may be more open to the inner voice of guidance and our path more easily guided.

To a certain extent, our lives are complex simply by virtue of being human. Yet we need not face the complexity alone, and we need not make life more complex than necessary. Much of our complexity is self-imposed, either to keep up with a goal that isn't even ours or to fill up empty spaces left by pain and trauma. With help from our angels, we can choose to let go of that old pain and trauma and keep only that which moves us forward. Their purpose is to provide us support and guidance in this and many other areas, if we only seek it.

Reflection

Consider that humans were created to be complex in order to learn soul lessons. How does this resonate with your current beliefs and activities?

_____

_____

_____

_____

If you feel your life is currently too complex, how can you embrace connection as a way to find more simplicity?

_____

_____

_____

_____

Balance Within

You look across this human life between
Right and Wrong
Black and White
Good and Bad
Life and Death
and howl in roaring discontent
for lives well-spent in others' cages

Yet all things bear extremes
and in-betweens
In the gray is where the magic happens:
humanity comes alive,
peace is sought and won,
lives laid down for one another

Your days of love's labor
are not long for this world
The distance between heaven and hell
becomes but a speck of dust
you carry in your pocket
along the uneasy, winding way to dusk's door
and dawn's welcoming embrace

It is difficult to live both a divine life and a worldly life. Yet, this is our task as humans. At our core, we are spirit, and at the same time, we exist in the world. We must live in the world. For generations, humans have been in a state of doing, and those who have succeeded in this lifestyle have attempted to encourage all others to follow their path. As a result, in large part, the world is very focused on doing all the time. We often see those who live at a slower pace, who prefer to balance doing with being, as weaker, as a people easy to conquer, marginalize, or ignore.

This time is no more. A new energy is moving into the world. Though it seems new to us, it actually has existed since the beginning of time. Source energy and human energy, are like two sides of the same coin. There is the doing (masculine) energy and the being (feminine) energy. Within the Source, this energy is balanced. When we return to Source after our physical deaths, we experience this balanced energy once again. However, on Earth, masculine doing energy has reigned for centuries, and the result is what we see around us: people too busy to care about each other, rampant consumerism, corporations running governments, corruption, poverty, isolation, depression, illness, wars; the list goes on and on. All this great suffering can be counterbalanced with feminine energy. Feminine energy possesses the understanding of stillness, connection, acceptance, slowing down, and peace.

We must find the balance that allows us to become open to the Divine, while not losing our grounding in the world. We must stop trying to fill our voids with worldly things, with only doing, for we find the Divine in the empty places. The places we dare not go for fear of what we may find or feel – that is where we connect to the Source and the Divine within and find our balance.

Reflection

How do you understand the concept of "doing" versus "being"?

_____

_____

_____

_____

How do you feel this understanding of finding greater balance through connection benefits you?

_____

_____

_____

_____

Spiritual Abundance

A day late, a dollar short
What if you show up for the world like that?
Dragging behind you all your many things,
The people you've collected,
All the time you've wasted,
The world at your feet
And you don't even see it.

Running this way and that
Still looking for more,
Showing up yet rarely slowing down,
You feel the silence like grit between your teeth,
Spitting it out like tobacco.

That's our grit in there, they say,
Our grit that polishes you to a shiny stone
And you cast it away,
Watch it form a pillar on the ground
While you carry on with your unpolished ways,
Searching, always searching,
For what's already there,
Available for the taking

Abundance does not mean acquiring lots of stuff. We will always have a need or want; we may not have as much as someone else has. This is the beautiful imperfection and variety of being human. These differences simultaneously set us apart and have the power to bring us closer together. They only show up as lack if we perceive them that way. Moreover, when we constantly focus on this lack, we often overlook all that we do have.

Part of our journey is to develop skills to meet our human needs in a creative way. Perhaps this is actually receiving the object of our desire. Perhaps it is realizing that we can do without or using ingenuity to find an alternative solution. Perhaps our need is tied with someone else's and we have the opportunity to collaborate with another person to meet that shared need. There are so many possibilities. The best possible solution is that in the end, whether we fill the need or not, we realize the Creator is the source of all abundance and therefore abundance is not a material object. No amount of material objects in the world can make us abundant humans.

True abundance comes from knowing our connection to our angels and to the Creator, from accepting our spiritual nature as our real lives. When we do this, perception of lack dissipates. We are more comfortable with what we have because this experience is temporary, while we recognize that we are infinite.

Reflection

How does this challenge your concept of abundance?

_____

_____

_____

_____

How can you use connection to see lack differently?

_____

_____

_____

_____

Healing from Within

*In the deepest, darkest recesses
There resides a space
For only you*

*A space where you may enter and dwell,
To rest and receive the blessings
That are your gift*

*Where you may receive the guidance
That is our promise to you,
A promise made before time began,*

*Made in holy space
Signed in spirit
Sealed in angel's wings*

A promise for your everlasting care,
That you may not go this path alone,
That when you seek home

And the company of those whom you left
So many lives ago, you may connect
Through the silent space within

That open, lonely space waits to be filled
That love, that place
Only found within

If you seek, if you open,
If you allow the light
Into the empty spaces

Our angels offer us healing from within. Their voices can guide us and help us to make good decisions. Their heavenly energy can help heal our darkest wounds. They help us to be the best person we can be while we are here on earth.

Like rain, the angels cleanse our tears, our hurts, and our deepest pain. They heal the spiritual body so that the physical may thrive. So many people need healing. They are so far away from connection and as a result are sick. For many, it is not a physical illness; it is the spiritual illness of disconnection. It is the hardest part of being human, this seeming disconnection from the Creator. This is why the angels are with us. They help bridge that gap.

Their love, their devotion is always available and their purpose is to guide us in this world. They do this through our prayers, through our requests for their assistance. They cannot intrude without our permission. Yes, sometimes people seem to be saved in miraculous ways. That may be part of their larger purpose, or it may serve another, unseen purpose. We do not usually know their story. We must focus only on our story. Asking the angels for help daily greatly improves our happiness and our ability to fulfill our own story and healing. We all have a reason we are here. The healing we do helps us to fulfill that purpose, or in some cases, hinders its progress. The angels' assistance helps keep us on track.

Reflection

Consider the concept of "spiritual illness of disconnection." How does this give new insight to conventional ideas around illness and healing?

_____

_____

_____

_____

How do you think disconnection relates to what is happening with people in the world today?

_____

_____

_____

_____

True Purpose

*It gets to you eventually,
Though you may pretend
You don't hear the siren song
Running for too long only smashes
You into the neon sign
That was waiting for you anyway*

*You may selfishly chase other ideas
Only to realize you are nothing more
Than a dog barking after its own tail
Round and round in circles you go*

*Until you finally listen to the innate language
Of the spirit inside, which calls you
To your higher purpose, guides you
Through the most dimly lit corridors
And sun-bathed expanses,
Shelters in the times of greatest need*

You can avoid and hide
Yet until you set your life aside
And atone to inner wisdom
Intuition will seek you out
Find you in your most hidden places
And if you allow, direct you
To the purpose of your being

We all have a purpose. For some of us, there may be one specific role to play in this lifetime. For others, it may be a general direction in life that can be fulfilled through various jobs and actions. For still others, there may be many different paths all culminating in the same overall purpose. Our purpose could be very small or very large. All actions have the potential to lead to our true purpose, even if they seem off course.

We may have strayed early; however it's never too late to move in the right direction. We can develop our special skills and gifts to the world at any time we're ready, and many choices can all lead to the same path eventually. This is what the angels do; they help us recognize our calling and make choices in the direction that will move us onto our path. That gentle nudging is our angels, whispering to our hearts.

Sometimes guidance is difficult. Sometimes it seems what we're asked to do is downright impossible. Yet we are called to do it because someone or some situation needs our particular gifts, even if we don't know what that means. Even if we can't see yet what we bring to the world, the angels do and they guide us toward opportunities to use our unique gifts.

We must not despair if others criticize us. As humans, we can't expect to receive appreciation for everything we do. Our path is growth and sometimes criticism or derision is the lesson that keeps us headed in the right direction. If we give up on something because the world is not impressed, we may miss our calling altogether. We must allow ourselves to persevere, even in the face of criticism, if we feel the familiar tug of spirit edging us toward our path. That is the angels' job, to help guide us on our way and keep us fulfilling what we are here to do. When we commune with them, we find the guidance we seek.

Reflection

How do you hear the angel inside whispering or nudging you toward your path?

_____

_____

_____

_____

_____

How can you move past criticism to stay on the path?

_____

_____

_____

_____

_____

Nourishing Relationships

What if I'm the angel beside you,
Wings tucked tightly
Into street clothes,
Unassuming yet wholly connected
To the one?

What if it's your neighbor,
The one who leaves the holiday lights
Strung up for months?
What if he has more important work to do?

Perhaps it's the homeless man
Who asks for your last dollar,
Or the woman who cuts you off in traffic?
How will you react?

What if the world is full of angels,
Bringing light to people everywhere,
Disguised as one of you?

We each have a human family and a spiritual family. Our human family keeps us connected to our humanity, to who we are in this lifetime. Even if we don't like them, are estranged from them, or consider friends who are not blood-related to be more like our family, these people are the ones who make us human. Our connection with them keeps us grounded and keeps us on our daily path.

Our human connections are helpers on this path; we must not take their importance lightly. Even the ones who hurt us may actually help us through the experience of pain and forgiveness. However, when we become too mired in the human life we often neglect our divine purpose, the purpose that our angels exist to help us fulfill.

Human relationships are difficult; the angels understand that. It is one of our greatest challenges in this life. For some, it is simply our purpose to find balance in this area. For others, we must find balance and transcend this struggle to move on to tasks that are more important. We all have a divine purpose. Everyone is important to this world.

Having only human connections keeps us from our spiritual path, from the purpose we have here on earth. We must see to it that we nourish our spiritual relationships as well as our human ones, for we are both human and divinely spirit at once. Yet we are only human for a short while. We are spirit forever. Spiritual relationships are not complicated. They do not come with human limitations, like jealousy, anger, and greed. They are true, unconditional soul love from the Source, a gift to all people who seek it. There is no need to wait until death of our physical forms. We can receive this gift now and experience the peace of the spirit any time we want through connection with our angels.

Benefits of Connecting

Reflection

How might you cultivate spiritual relationships as a human?

_____

_____

_____

_____

_____

What areas of your human relationships may need attention to ensure they support your spiritual growth?

_____

_____

_____

_____

_____

Co-Creation with Spirit

*Inside you there lies a new life
Waiting to be born
A tiny, breathing creation
Feeding on your life-blood,
Absorbing your deepest desires,
Becoming the whole of you*

*Let it out.
Let it breathe the squalid air,
Taste the harshness of the world,
Shine its beauty over the decay
Of modern man.
Let it be free in this world,
Allow it to share its healing gifts,
Created in the womb of your own soul*

Our thoughts and ideas are a gift from the Creator. It's not that we can't or don't think plenty on our own. Much of the time, our human thoughts crowd out those inspired at a spiritual level. This is again why a connection with the angels is helpful. They can help us discern between thoughts of a human nature and those derived from spiritual energy. Both are necessary, of course. Not every moment of our human lives requires spiritual inspiration. However, we are made in the image of the Creator, and as such, we are also a creator. Our thoughts and ideas are the start of the creative process.

When we open ourselves to spiritual guidance, creative thoughts and ideas flow more naturally and align with our unique purpose and desires. This not to say we cannot originate great ideas on our own. We are intelligent beings. Nevertheless, human ideas include the risk of being more selfish or self-serving when they are not lovingly guided by spirit. We may avoid our path because it isn't the easiest route, and in doing so follow our own ideas. We may have a wildly successful life by human standards. And we may be happy. However, there is deeper happiness and fulfillment that comes from following our spiritual calling and it requires being open to spiritual guidance.

The angels will never force us to do anything. Instead, they may guide us to create in ways that are out of our comfort zone. That is part of the process for many.

Sometimes our path is about stretching to new areas. If it looks easy for others, we need not worry. Sometimes our path is difficult to reach, particularly if we've strayed far in our lives. Once we get through the difficult parts and start connecting, co-creation becomes easier, natural, like it is meant to be – because it is.

Reflection

Consider that being made by a divine Creator, you are also a creator. How does this inform your concept of creativity?

_____

_____

_____

_____

How can you start to discern between your own thoughts and the guidance from your angel inside?

_____

_____

_____

_____

Minimized Suffering

*When the darkest sky
Lights your existence,
When you feel the gravity
Caving in on your soul,
Know that you are never,
Ever alone*

*We are here, always watchful,
Always waiting for you to reach out
Ask for us
With great open arms,
We welcome you*

*To the peace of the source
To the life of the light
That shines on the darkest days,
That no amount of suffering can dim*

For with us, suffering is an illusion
And pain a distant dream
Our arms, a place of hope
Our voices, a retreat from earthly toils

In the darkest of moments,
When chaos and pain swirl around you,
There is an angel who reaches for you.
Take her hand,
And let her guide you to peace.

Part of our experience as humans is to experience unrest, disconnection, and struggle. Although this is not for punishment or to learn a lesson, we do always have the opportunity to grow from the experience when and if we are ready. However, many of us get mired in the struggle. The angels can help us see suffering in a different way. These experiences can help us find success on our path. Without them, we would not be able to share our knowledge and experiences with others, which, in turn, helps them to grow.

If the concept of learning from suffering and pain is challenging, consider that we are our souls, our spirits, first. We leave the Creator to become temporarily human, where we have a variety of experiences. While human, we have the choice to transform our experiences into personal growth and learning opportunities. What we experience as humans is limited in comparison to the eternal nature of our souls, precisely to minimize the suffering. Our real home is the energy and love of the Creator, and eventually we return there. As we embrace connection, the angels can help us transform suffering into growth, simple actions into a life path, and basic human existence into soul expansion.

Though there will always be struggle, it is not in our spiritual nature to continually be sad, depressed, or defeated. These are human emotions and experiences, influenced largely by the hectic and disconnected lives we lead. We have the capacity, even while we are human, to be governed by love, joy, and peace if we are willing to give ourselves over to it. The angels know this is difficult. Yet each person who chooses to reduce suffering and seek peace contributes to the peace of the world. Just one human gesture toward love can impact many. Each person who chooses this path walks with the energy of the Creator to help eradicate suffering and bring the world back into balance. The angels can help transcend and dissolve our suffering through connection with the Source.

Reflection

Can you see struggle as an opportunity and suffering as a symptom of disconnection?

_____

_____

_____

_____

_____

If so, how does this change your views on the struggles and challenges in your life or in the world around you?

_____

_____

_____

_____

_____

Transition to Wholeness

*The wicked finality of life
is almost more beautiful than birth,
the grace and forcefulness
with which the body unbinds
from the constraints of humanity,
each day, slowing more and more,
the measured breaking down of flesh and ego,
a thinning of the veil
which shrouds the spirit from its home.*

*Until one day you see it in their eyes;
you know they have seen Home
and they are ready
and you are ready
to let go as they have.*

*Oh, the cruel and terrible dichotomy of grief,
to hold your beloved, to never want to let loose
your connection, yet to look death in the face
and know surrender is the only promise
for true salvation and peace for both.*

Like walking outside on a brisk fall day,
naked as trees,
wearing only the cloak of nature's chill,
allow the tears to flow in colorful waves
as leaves fall, purposefully,
with finality and hope,
rotting on the ground
through the dormancy of winter,
only to regenerate new life
when the sun once again warms the skin.

Your liberation may not come until years later,
when you can finally take comfort
in the distance between suffering and release,
when you can set up your altar
and place your heart there
to be cleansed and unburdened,
light the candle, assemble the stones and blessings
in the order that sets things right
for your spirit to grieve,
and then leave it there exposed,
to be encased in love and peace
until it is your time
to also begin the journey Home.

Our experience of death is often misguided. We see it as separation when instead it is a reconnection with the Source. Though we are physically separated from our human companions, energetically we are closer than we've ever been, because the truest connection is at the soul level. The only way to experience this fully is through physical death, which is the barrier of the soul. Therefore, we can mourn when someone dies and also rejoice that their soul is reunited with the Source of all life, the one who makes us whole, who supplies us with unending love and purpose in this life and the life beyond.

When we die, the angels are there to welcome us with open arms. After a human lifetime served together, they are the first of many to welcome us home, regardless of how we get there. There is no good or bad death, there is only our path. Sometimes we may stray; we may make choices that lead to suffering and more choices that are unfulfilling. There may be actions we take in our human life that seem unkind or even downright evil. Connection to your angels can mitigate all these and more.

Human life is full of mistakes. It's ideal that we learn from and resolve them while still in our physical bodies; however, if we don't there is still hope after physical death. The Creator is loving and forgiving and only wants our highest good. It helps us remember that we are spirit forever and always; we are only human for a relatively short time. This human life, this human pain, these human choices are temporary. They are not who we are.

Inside, our perfect spiritual nature has already made us whole.

Reflection

How does this expand your view on death?

_____

_____

_____

_____

How does this expand your view on forgiveness?

_____

_____

_____

_____

Part 3: How to Connect

Retreat Inward

Sit
Sit quietly and allow yourself
To take up residence in your own skin
Let the lighted sage clear away
All the congestion of a life
Filled too full
Played down to the wire

Breathe in the sacred smoke
Breathe out the swirling negativity
That fills each cell
Allow only peace and calm to remain
Allow the warm candlelight
To take you adrift
Into the ocean of your being
Your spirit, your essence
the captain on your journey
into the higher voyage
of the soul

Let go
Let go and float
Bodiless and mindless
Floating on the waves of being
Until you sense the connection
The reconnection
To all that you are
All that you were
All that you ever will be

Sit quietly
Let go
Float in the ocean of your being

We have so many opportunities to reach our angels. The greatest is silence or meditation. The angels can be found so easily when we quiet our minds. So many of us have difficulty making time for ourselves like this or being able to quiet our minds even for a few minutes.

When we want to reach our angels, we can sit quietly and burn a candle. We can close our eyes and allow our minds to become still. And then we can listen, feel, sense. We can choose not to react or expect. We can just be. Sometimes we will notice our angels and other times we will not. We mustn't be discouraged. Over time and with practice we will reach them, if we so desire. The angels have been connected to us since we came to Earth, watching over us and helping us as we need it. They are our guides, our protectors, and we must ask for and be open to their help.

Consistency is key. If we only connect every now and then, it will be difficult each time and we may lose interest out of frustration. Connecting often builds a skill, like a sport. The more we practice, the better we get and the easier it is to connect. Connecting deliberately in quiet moments also helps build our skill in hearing our angels during other parts of our day, for they do not reach out to us only during meditation. However, most of our lives are so busy that it's difficult to recognize their messages amidst all our activity. Quiet time helps us start to become aware of how they speak and how we hear them, so we can discern their voices at any time. This is important, because most of us do not have more than five or ten minutes in a day for meditation, where an hour or more would be ideal. If we can learn to hear our angels at other times, they can offer us more guidance throughout our day.

Reflection

Where in your day can you start to build in short periods of time for meditation or even just silence?

_____

_____

_____

_____

What methods can you employ to ensure consistency in your practice?

_____

_____

_____

_____

_____

Silence the Mind

*Nothing comes
and when nothing comes
what is left?*

*There is the stillness
that fills the spaces in between thoughts
and action,
the spaces that spur
movement
or paralyze in fear*

*When nothing comes
you have no choice
but to go there*

*To seek rather than be sought
to find the knowing
that is buried
in plain sight*

*the golden light
of creation energy
and the stillness of the places
in between...*

*...to create something
from nothing*

If we find silence or meditation to be too difficult, we can simply be still. We spend so much time busy, often with unfulfilling or unnecessary tasks. We fill every day, every hour, every second with something. When is it time for our own self-care? When is it time for us to go within? We must make the time to still the world around us— to disconnect, turn off noise that isn't natural, put down anything in our hands that may distract, and just be still. Sit right there in our kitchen with no TV, no phone, no dishwasher running. What might we hear?

We can listen to the sounds around us that we normally miss because of all the other noise. Then, if we dare, we can listen for our own voice, the silent voice that speaks the loudest. Is it filling us with fear? That voice, that is fearful, is our gatekeeper, the one that keeps us rooted in the physical world. She wants to protect us, yet in her haste, she has kept us from a great gift. We can let her share her fears and not immediately accept them as truth. Once she realizes we are ready, her voice will subside, and another will emerge. This is the voice of stillness, of life-giving nourishment, of connection to that which is both within us and larger than we are. It is our window to the universe and to our very souls, and we will find it in stillness.

Stillness is good for connecting with our angels; it is healthy for us to have time to slowdown, to retreat inside. There we find answers, respite, and peace. If we do not choose stillness, it may eventually be chosen for us. Life events have a way of getting us what we need most, often in ways that seem painful or unfair. Even then, we must accept the stillness that is offered to us. It cannot be forced. Stillness is a choice, and it is important to make it daily– it is important for us, for those we love, and for the world. If we want to help the world, we must find stillness within ourselves.

Reflection

How often do you allow yourself to really be still? What keeps you from it?

_____

_____

_____

_____

_____

Have you experienced "forced stillness," life events that require you to slow down due to stress, pain, illness, etc.?

_____

_____

_____

_____

_____

Practice Gratitude

*Love what you have
For the good things will come
When you least expect,
Though not when you are busy loathing
that which you already possess*

*Love what you have,
Both the joys and challenges
Brought with life,
For your worth is not made of
Things or people or situations,
But rather the love you bring to each,
The grace with which you encounter
Both the joys and unpleasantries*

The vessel will find itself with many cracks
And struggle to stay full in life,
Each setback creating
a new spiderweb of compromise
To the foundation that is the very core
which bears a stable life

Yet the one who wisely fills in the cracks with gold
May still hold water, nourishing self and others
With the cool drink of loving-kindness

The one who loves the cracks
As part of the whole,
Sees the beauty and power
Of brokenness
And reconciliation

The importance of gratitude in connecting cannot be understated. Gratitude helps build the bridge between us and our angels. Gratitude is a reaching out, a way of connecting to our angels with our thoughts and feelings. A humble and gracious heart is more willing to be open to guidance from the unseen forces around us, more invested in and open to connection. Our angels are grateful to be in communion with us, to help where they are needed. Our gratitude for their love and guidance, our connection with them, is our gift in return.

Even in times of great unrest, we can find peace and connection through gratitude. Even when storms seem to swirl all around us, when the people of the world all seem to be at war, we can find hope and peace with our angels. When people are oppressed or acting as an oppressor, our angels can show us the peace and freedom of the Creator. When our personal world is in turmoil, they are here. Even when everything is well, when the world seems to be righting itself and the rockiness of human life is temporarily smoothed, they are still here, ready for us to call on them. There is power in connecting even in good times. It's easy to call on something bigger than we are when things seem to be falling apart. However, we strengthen our connection when we call out during stable times as well.

Each day, we can light a candle, sit quietly, and consider all in our lives for which we can be grateful. We find in this simple practice that we have much more good in our lives than perhaps we even recognize, and we find that we are slowly, yet distinctly, forming a connection with our angels. Our daily practice of gratitude can be done anywhere at any time, with or without a candle. We can simply imagine the flame in our mind's eye, glowing brightly, reminding us of the unseen but very real connection of our angels, waiting for us, loving us, grateful for our connection.

Reflection

Do you regularly practice gratitude? What practices do you use?

_____

_____

_____

_____

How does gratitude feel different during stable times and difficult times?

_____

_____

_____

_____

Let Go

You search your whole life
For your purpose, your path
You climb the mountains
Ask the questions
Get the degrees
Cry in the night for the answers
Until you feel it's a lost cause,
The answer isn't for you

But child, it is
And seeking is not the path
You must listen
And be still
And open your eyes
To what is right in front of you
And all around you

Your destiny lies in who you are,
What you love,
The passion that gets you
Fiery and red-hot inside
The joy that you bring
Not just to others
But also to yourself

Open up
Take in the spirit that is calling
The breath of life moves through you
Each moment
Reveals your passion
Brings you joy
Gives you purpose
Guides your path
Whispers that you are enough,
And that is all you ever need to be

Forgiveness is another path to connection and healing. We often experience forgiveness as a double-edged sword. We are told to forgive those who hurt us for our own growth, yet sometimes the wound is too deep or has happened too recently. We are not ready to forgive. Yet we can always choose to let go. We can let go of the guilt and shame we carry—that which we put on ourselves and that which we have accepted from others. Guilt and shame are heavy and often keep us mired in the human experience, making us feel disconnected from our angels and from the Creator. When we let go, we give ourselves freedom from this weight.

Forgiveness and letting go are light. They allow us to separate ourselves from the desperation that feeling unworthy brings. Once free and forgiving of ourselves, we may eventually feel ready to forgive others for their humanness when and if the time is right. Or we may not. Either way, we lessen our burden and increase our ability to connect.

Additionally, many human belief systems include the need to ask for forgiveness from past bad behaviors and for being imperfect. Certainly, if we have hurt or harmed others it is wise and compassionate to ask them for forgiveness in order to fortify our relationship with them and to help with our own growth. And it is good to ask the Creator and our angels for forgiveness as well. We must also remember that the trials and mistakes we experience are part of being human. Inside, our perfect spiritual nature, made in the image of the Creator, has already made us whole. We do not have to ask forgiveness for being imperfect. We can simply forgive ourselves and the Creator will feel it too. All people will feel it, for we are all connected in the light.

Reflection

How does this concept of forgiveness differ from your upbringing or beliefs?

_____

_____

_____

_____

How do you see the practice of forgiveness helping to connect your spiritual and human sides?

_____

_____

_____

_____

Support Well-being

Ebbing and flowing,
Cleansing and nourishing,
From the tiniest fish that swim in your veins,
to the largest whales of your soul,
rely on the life-giving water from within,
nourished by the sun through day,
Directed by the tides at night,
touched by the hand of God
and bestowed the power
To create and sustain life,
to raise up great storms
and inspire the heart of man,
To love with great fury and tear down walls
Built long ago by another people's war

*The water that makes you
Is ordained with holy wings
Harness the power of the great ocean inside,
Use it not for devastation
of the unruly and sinful parts,
but as a sacred trough
from which all may drink
and find the blessings of life*

Our connection to our angels is energetic and ethereal, and it is also in many ways physical. It helps to have a strong physical body in order to reach them. Our bodies are precious temples, and as such, we are called to keep them healthy and functioning properly. This includes loving the bodies in which we live. We should strive to take care of our temples, for that helps us connect with our angels. When our bodies are healthy, our minds are more likely to be clear from fogginess, worry, and stress, and we are better able to connect.

When we are overly tired, drinking too much, taking a variety of medication, even eating too much, it can affect our ability to connect. Our minds become cloudy, our energy is affected and our angels may seem distant from us. When we feel bad, it's often harder to connect because we are distracted with the pain or discomfort. Taking steps to lessen this can help us in our connection.

Each of us exists in a body that needs something for its greatest health: different foods, different drinks, and different levels of exercise. We can spend time exploring what works best for our unique bodies and what makes us feel well. We can listen to our bodies' cues, which are connected to the guidance from our angels. Our bodies will let us know what is working and what isn't.

Our angels know that good health is a challenge in this time. Much has been done to pollute our air, our water, and our food sources. There is much confusion over what is healthy and what is not. We can't focus too much on what we should or shouldn't eat or do. We must listen to our inner guidance and make small changes until we feel better. We must explore alternatives that fit simply into our lifestyles and support our overall well-being. As we take steps to clear our minds with silence, we can also take steps to clear our bodies and lives of the things they don't need.

Reflection

Have you noticed any subtle signs that your body may need something different to be at its best?

_____

_____

_____

_____

Understanding that everyone's highest good is different and everyone is on a different path in this life, how might you apply the concept of improved health as a benefit of connecting?

_____

_____

_____

_____

Move Mindfully

In the glow
In the flow

Your heavenly light illuminates
Shines
Uncovers
The inner glow of a thousand lives

Joys real
Sorrows piercing
Engaged and enlivened
By the one true light

Encapsulated and free
Time-bound and timeless
Dancing on a moonbeam
With stars as fiery hair

A millennium of song caressing old bones
Into entranced movement

Let the dance not waiver
Let the music never cease

Movement is the natural way of the body, and ignoring this important area impacts personal well-being, which can impede connection. We need movement in our lives.

We must make moving a priority. We can move every day, even if all we do is get up and walk around our office or our home a few times. So many of us sit all day in sedentary jobs. We increasingly feel sluggish and tired. Sitting all day creates a sense of stagnancy that can hinder connection. Movement gets the blood and lymph flowing in our bodies, cleansing our systems and regenerating us. It creates energy, invigorating our bodies and our souls.

Movement should be enjoyable. We can have fun and listen to the guidance of our bodies! If movement is new for us, we can start slowly and not push ourselves too hard. We can find ways to make movement sacred. We can engage in mindfulness as we move, observing flowers, people, clouds, animals, or the movement itself. Practices like yoga or dance often incorporate sacred or spiritual movements and can be a great option for us. Movement that is purposeful, meaningful, and intentional helps bring health to our bodies, and therefore better connection to our angels.

Reflection

What are your thoughts about the role of movement in connection?

_____
_____
_____
_____
_____

Do you get enough movement in your daily life? If not, how can you incorporate more movement into your days?

_____
_____
_____
_____
_____

Engage in Creative Expression

With your hands, build the future
One tiny piece of wire or brick
Or drop of paint at a time

With your heart, love the world well
Each hug, each kind gesture,
Each forgiveness
One step closer to redemption

With your spirit, become the essence
Of the world you want to see,
Embody the Creator
In your every thought,
In your soul's flow,

So that Earth in its tragedy
May embody Heaven
On its hill of salvation
Reachable, connecting,
A shining light of hope

Our Creator has bestowed the power of creating into each one of us. When we are creating, we are tapping into the power of the Source and therefore our angels. If we have not found our creative niche, it is important that we do so. It does not have to be art, music, or writing, although those are worthwhile creative endeavors that anyone can do. There is no requirement to be good at it, only to be inspired by it. We must find the creative activity that we enjoy and that inspires us—that will help bring us closer to Source.

Creative expression also allows us to clear stagnant energy, pent up frustration, anger, or pain carried around in our bodies, minds, and souls, which can hinder our connection to our angels. The sense of release found in creating provides the strength and motivation to continue. As we work, the energy of frustration is replaced by the energy of accomplishment, creation, and transformation.

In addition, creative expression is manual and experiential. We are active participants, physically making the transformation possible. Engaging in a creative activity, we may find ourselves energized, relishing in the freedom and creativity of our labor, the joy of unbridled personal expression, and the opening of the connection with our angels.

Reflection

What kinds of creative activities do you enjoy? Which ones feel more spiritual to you, leading to connection?

_____

_____

_____

_____

How can you mindfully carve out time for you to engage in creative expression on a regular basis?

_____

_____

_____

_____

Experience Nature

The peace of the willows
Is found in the gentle cool breezes
As they pass through each blade
Swishing softly to produce
A safe haven where the mind
Can rest at the end of a weary day

Rest by the water's edge,
Trickling stream navigating
Over life's rocky challenges
To flow on, around the bends
And turns, through darkness
And light to the vast delta
Of understanding, faith, and hope
Where all life comes together,
As far as the eyes can see
As deep as the heart can feel

Rest there, waves lapping at your feet
Allow the pull to take you under
Make you one with their gentle lullaby,
The warm breezes,
The vast expanse which tugs At you,
begging for connection,
the peace, love, and the light of your soul

Nature is the purest form of spiritual existence and therefore an especially good way to reach our angels. It operates solely by universal laws with no interventions or interference. All natural entities respect the laws and abide by them. They follow the cycles set forth without complaint or alteration. Nature does not adapt the world around it to its liking; rather it adapts itself to the universal laws, cycles, seasons, and inevitable fluctuations. And despite its lack of desire for power and domination, nature thrives. No matter how destroyed or displaced, if left on its own, nature regenerates gradually and unselfishly.

Our struggle with connection as humans is often directly related to a lack of reverence and respect for the natural world. The more we attempt to bypass natural laws and cycles, the more distanced we become, for we are playing God, and though we possess the spirit of the Creator, we are not the Creator. We are created, just like the nature humans seek to overpower or destroy. As such, we can use the natural world to help us with connecting to our angels.

Because of its purity, nature is a perfect channel. In very few other places can we be closer to spirit while in human form. Angels are all around, speaking to us if we will listen. We can immerse ourselves, feel the energy, and observe the symbiosis, the harmonies of nature. We can touch the trees, the leaves, the grass, smell the flowers, and feel the wind. Even if it seems strange, we can do it anyway. Renewed practice in nature and respect for all living things– be they people, animals, or plants– is extremely helpful in connecting. Nature's energy is the angels' energy. Nature's respect for cycles and laws is reflected through our angels. Nature's closeness with the Source brings us closer as well.

Reflection:

Do you spend enough time in nature? If not, how can you ensure you get more of this important means of connection?

_____

_____

_____

_____

How have you experienced nature or animals as a source of spiritual connection or inspiration?

_____

_____

_____

_____

Explore the Senses

Do you see the signs around you?
Do you catch the subtleties
Of human form and language,
The gestures that, though invisible,
May signify the change that is to come?

Do you feel it in your bones,
Like an ache that cannot be quenched
With all the fire in the universe,
Yet softens with only love touch?

Do you run in quiet fields
With tall grass, listening to the whisper
As each blade glides against another
As your feet swish in the underbrush
Stepping to the time of nature's rhythm?

Do you laugh as if a child,
With the freedom and grace that is confidence
In endless tomorrows
And eternal play?

Do you gather all the signs,
Hold them close to your body
In the place where love enters you,
Shout forgiveness and gratitude
And fiery tears into the blackened sky,
Counting every blessing, every gift,
Every challenge that brought you to your knees,
Raise hands to tomorrow,
Whatever that may be,
Whatever you may become?

The doing, being, forgiving, honoring,
laughing, loving, crying
Do you see the signs?

We have available to us five basic senses with which to explore our world. So many of us use these senses only to explore the world immediately around us— that which we can touch, see, hear, smell, or taste. Yet there are layers. The world is made up of that which cannot be so easily recognized, and the basic senses can be used to detect the layers beyond what is commonly accepted or acknowledged.

We must spend some time exploring how we best sense the world around us. We can use our strongest physical senses to help connect to our angels. If we tend to be visual, we can start to pay attention to visual clues around us. We can look for things out of the ordinary, things other people may not see, things we've not noticed before. These could be feathers, repeating numbers, pennies, or something else that is meaningful to us. If our strongest sense is touch, we can pay attention to the sensations around us. How does the energy feel different from room to room, person to person? If hearing is dominant, we can pay attention to sounds in the same way we notice visuals or touch. At first, we may be overly sensitive and not everything we sense will be a message or a connection. Over time and with practice though, our senses will sharpen and we will be able to discern more easily.

We also must consider our more subtle senses, such as gut feelings or intuition. These may not be part of our five physical senses, yet they are very real and powerful. Our intuition and feelings give us clues that we may be ignoring physically. We can listen and trust. That intuition is both our inner wisdom and an expression of the Creator and our angels, giving us guidance. Although they can share, they can't make us listen or act. We must use these gifts to our benefit, as they can empower us to make good decisions to keep us happy, peaceful, and possibly even safe.

Reflection

What is your strongest sense? How do you pick up practical messages in your everyday life that can be expanded to grow your ability to connect?

_____

_____

_____

_____

Do you listen to your intuition and feelings for messages? If not, how can you start to pay more attention?

_____

_____

_____

_____

Cultivate Love

A gentle web connects us all,
Stretched far across
All time and space,
Each strand built
With godstuff and angel light,
Remaining dim until you reach out,
Make the connection,
Light up the thread,
Take the hand that reaches toward you

Though it may be different
Though it may be disfigured
Though it may be indigent or wealthy
Thought it may be full of hatred

How To Connect

Grasp it tightly
Don't let go
Until every strand burns brightly
Until the darkness is lit
And love becomes the way
Weaving through all

Love, the connection
That binds all beings as One

The ultimate act of connection is through love. When we express love of any kind— love for people we already know, love for people we struggle with, love for animals, love for the earth, love for ourselves—we are connecting with our angels. Even if we are not aware, when we love, we are one with them.

If we are unsure of what to do, we can start with cultivating love. We can ask, "Who or what do I love most? When I feel love most strongly, what am I doing? Who am I with?" Love for material objects or money won't bring us closer. Expanding our capacity to love the life around us will.

It's easy to love those around us who we care about. It's easiest to practice expanding that love in order to expand our connection with the angels. However, that is just the tip of the iceberg. To really expand and enhance our capacity for love, and therefore to connect with our angels, we must learn to love all creation, all beings, even the most unlovable. Even ourselves. This requires a great deal of compassion and empathy and a willingness to set aside judgments and shame. This requires us to see all beings as the Creator sees them— wholly loved as the perfect beings they are. The Creator does not see any of us and regret the act of creating. Yes, we as a people have evolved far away from the Light, and that is why the angels are reaching out to us, to help bring us home. There are many paths that can bring us back around; the most powerful path is love.

Reflection

In what ways can you cultivate the feeling of love for all beings, including yourself and the world around you?

_____

_____

_____

_____

What are your thoughts and personal challenges about loving and accepting everyone as the Creator does—as perfect and whole, without judgment?

_____

_____

_____

_____

Part 4: The Journey Forward

The Time is Near

The time is near when you will hear the whisper
When you will heed the song
When you will throw your pretense to the sky
And let you heart wander free

Free to release the stirrings inside
Hold them in peace and give them light to grow

Free to open to the connection
That is your birthright, your Divine gift
Your alter to the Source of unconditional love
You can't lose it -- it's inside you

The time is near when you will feel
Allow yourself to be cut
in order to experience the light
Instead of always running
into the arms of darkness
Trying to numb out the lightest sting

One day you will call on us
And we will be your heavenly beacon
Your burning light of refuge
As you make your way through this life

The time is near
The time is near

The Angel Inside

The time is near when we must make a choice. The world is changing fast. For generations, man has cultivated a life without a connection with angels. Miracles have become less obvious; angels are rarely spotted. That is now changing. Look at what our world has become without its connection to the Source. In order to continue the human race, we need this connection. We cannot continue to deny it or shun it as something bad.

All through human history, the great spiritual leaders understood this connection. They spoke of it in their teachings, they performed hundreds of miracles only possible with this connection, and yet over time we have lost this aspect of our spirituality and instead have accepted fear. The Creator is not fear-based. We are in no danger from the Creator if we do not choose connection. However, our human life will likely be more difficult. It may be difficult to overcome suffering, to find peace. We can look around us and see all the suffering. Some face hardships yet still cling to faith and hope, while others actively suffer and seem to have given up, accepting this as the way life is. There is so much of this kind of suffering today. And it saddens the angels because it does not need to be this way. There is hope. There is promise in connection with them.

This world needs people who have found the light, who have hope, and who can show others that they, too, can experience connection to their angels.

We don't have to become ministers and preach sermons. We only have to believe, and once we know our angels, our light will automatically shine, and we will be so filled with love that others will want what we have.

Reflection

Are you willing to make the choice to seek a connection with your angels?

_____

_____

_____

_____

How do you feel this personal connection may impact your life, and the lives of those around you?

_____

_____

_____

_____

The World is Changing

When the darkest sky lights your existence
When you feel gravity caving in on your soul
Know that you are never, never alone

We are here, always watchful
Always waiting for you
To reach out, to ask for us,

With great open arms we welcome you
To the peace of the Source
To the light that shines on darkest days
That no amount of suffering can dim.

For with us, suffering is an illusion
And pain a distant dream,
Our arms, a place of hope
Our voices, a retreat from earthly toils

The world around us is changing! People are becoming more spiritual. People are heeding the call that has always been in their hearts. There is a shift and people are feeling it. The angels are reaching out to us to give us that extra nudge, hoping one whispered word, one phrase may make a difference.

There is no more time to wait. As the world changes, the expression of being human must change too. The angels know that so many of us feel helpless to combat all that happens in a world which we often perceive as evil. Our connection to the angels is one way to combat the helplessness we feel.

Will connecting with them cause evil to cease? Not all at once; however, we can start with ourselves. For in the end, we are the only ones we can control anyway. When we reach toward spirit, our act of bravery has a subtle yet noticeable ripple effect. It's already being felt as millions connect to their angels inside. People are increasingly speaking out as they connect, for the world is becoming a safer place to be who we are meant to be. There is much danger and turmoil yet we have personal freedoms humans have never experienced. Unfortunately, this is not true in all areas of the earth, which makes this call even more important. We need this connection, as do people across the planet. For each one of us who reaches out, who believes, there are countless others who are unknowingly touched. For we are all one; what touches one, touches all.

The Angel Inside

Even if we choose not to connect with our angels, they will still be here. Their presence is not negated by our lack of belief or by our fear. They will be here, still loving us and they will help others who call. They will ensure that those who are ready and willing find connection with them. No one who is open will ever be left out. And those who are not ready will always, always have a special guide waiting.

The Journey Forward

Reflection

What do *you* need to convince you that angels are real?

___

___

___

___

What do *you* need to prove the angels' love, or the love of the Creator?

___

___

___

___

Waking Up

The peace of the light is upon you
Raise your hands to the earth
To the trees, to the skies
To the people across the lands
Who need your fearless embrace
Your peaceful mind

The oneness you build
Within your ignited heart
Builds the world in which
Tomorrows never end
And all the people Do-ing
Cease their tirades and their tyranny
Join hearts in peace and light
To become the Be-ing,
The one who connects us all with love

*Spread your wings
For each of you possess
The guardians' grace
The ability to rise up and hear
The voices, heed the call
In the light, all fear dissipates
And in love, the final battle won*

What does it mean to say the world is changing or a shift is happening? People describe it in different ways. Some say ancient energy that has been suppressed for generations is being opened up. Some say the veil, or doorway, between humans and the spiritual world, is getting thinner so that humans have more access. Some say it has to do with astrology, how the stars, moons, and other celestial bodies are now aligning throughout the universe and moving into a high energetic vibration.

All of these explanations may hold some truth. These are various ways to explain that angels are more accessible than ever. They have always been here; however, as a result of religious beliefs, human physiological makeup, science, the atmosphere, energy of the earth, and other effects, this connection has not seemed as readily available.

These changes have resulted in many people "waking up." We are starting to see past the consumerism and fierce independence that leads to selfishness, past the systems put in place that now harm many while allowing a very few to profit greatly, past the governments that value power over peace, past the institutions that preach a misguided sense of spirituality.

People are better able to see the fallacies of the past and are speaking out. For some, it is their life purpose. Others are joining in as they too are able to see more clearly. This is not a universal coup; it is, at its core, a world that is becoming more connected. When we are connected to each other and to the universal love of the Creator, we desire love and peace for ourselves and for the world in which we live.

Reflection

Where do you see evidence around you that people are "waking up"?

_____

_____

_____

_____

What are your thoughts on the changes happening in the world and your role in helping people to become more connected?

_____

_____

_____

_____

Heaven on Earth

*Connect me
To some nugget of truth or insight
That I may record it for the world to know
That I may spill it from sacred lips
Like a stream ever-flowing*

*And if the sound still falls
On deaf ears and eyes that are averted
From the vision in my soul*

*So then use me as the song
In their hearts
The breath when they
Are disconnected
The lonely howl of pain
When the darkness lasts too long*

*May I be the focal point
Of hopeful direction
A calming in the rage
A cooling in the heat*

*Let my life be a lamp in the fog
Starting first with me*

As the world changes, so do we. We have a choice in whether we go with it or fight it. If we go with the changes, life is much easier and there is less suffering in the end for ourselves and for others. While we may not be able to see that now, the angels promise that when we stop fighting the connection, human life will improve, especially our inner sense of peace and contentment.

Yet so many do fight it. All this fighting and hate we see now and throughout history is evidence of people fighting their true spiritual nature. We must let those people go the way they feel is right. Fighting against them in order to stop them is no different than what they're doing. This is not to say we should allow people to do harmful things to each other, animals or the earth. However, fighting leads to extremism on both sides and a lack of true connection for all.

Instead, we can go inside, find our connection to our angels, and use the strength, peace, and love we find to raise our personal energy, which will in turn raise the energy of everyone, since we are connected. We can focus on our own growth; we do not need to worry about others and their path. Some people will never change; this may be their role here, and that is acceptable. It is not our job to change others, merely to change ourselves, for we are the only ones we can control.

As we connect with our angels and work with them, our need to control and judge others diminishes, and as we grow personally, our happiness, peace, and joy expands.

Our capacity for love expands beyond what we can even imagine. As we connect, as we learn to accept and embrace love, as we learn to share it with our fellow humans our energy rises, as does the energy of those around us. One by one, we contribute to the shift in the world; we participate in creating a sense of heaven on earth.

Reflection

Do you fight connection? In what ways can you start to let go and explore the possibilities?

_____

_____

_____

_____

How can you let go of control or judgment of others in order to help usher in "heaven on earth"?

_____

_____

_____

_____

The Start of Something New

Final entry in the Book of Life
Yet the night is still young
Still time to dance among fireflies
Pluck stars from the sky and carry them around
As our own personal lanterns

Let our wings fly free
As birds and butterflies in the wind
Enjoy the fire in our last days
Free the souls held captive for so long

New life is on the horizon
With all the fear and unknown it brings
And joy, let's not forget the joy found
In freedom and change

Like the lifting up in prayer
Of a gentle loving heart
The body and mind opens to new wonders
Miracles, if you will
Facilitated by our willingness
To move forward through our fear
Connected to the mere possibility
Of eternity on the other side

The start of something new is always beautiful: a new year, a new career, a new marriage, a new relationship. The angels implore us to start something new with them—to see how life-changing it can be. We can strengthen our faith, broaden our outlook on the spiritual, connect with the Creator in a way we never thought possible. This gift is ours for the taking. All we have to do is ask.

The angels are constantly reaching out, and we must make time for connection, even for a short time each day. We must find the ways that work for us. We have offered examples, yet these are not all-inclusive. The ways to reach them are as endless as the drops in the sea. We have so many options, and our angels are waiting.

It's the dawn of a new day! The world is changing. The old ways of being are being replaced. It is so important in this time that more and more people realize this gift of connection and do not fear it. The world needs more loving people connected with their Creator to be present in the world. Simply connecting and radiating the love of the Source is enough to push change along more quickly.

We have lived in darkness for too long. Our angels are the bridge between light and darkness. There is no time to lose. Our spiritual being will live for eternity; however, our life as human beings is limited. Now is the time to reconnect in peace, truth, and love with the Light, with our Angel Inside.

The Journey Forward

Reflection

Are you willing to connect? To reclaim your peace, truth, light, and love that exists within?

_____

_____

_____

_____

What questions or concerns do you still have? What may be preventing you from fully opening to the angel inside?

_____

_____

_____

_____

_____

Afterword

The angel inside
Wishes to tell you a secret:

That yours is a life worth living
A dream worth having
That your very existence
Brightens the earth
In a way no other can
That the light inside your soul
Is not meant to be hidden
Or denied
It is your gift to the world

This life that you live now
Is your impact on humankind
A model for generations to come
Death will not absolve you
But rather, lift you into the night
A shining beacon for all who wish to follow

Afterword

Live this life well
Find your peace within
Do minimal harm
Right your wrongs whenever possible
Shine your beacon for those who struggle
Those who wrong you
Those who are difficult to understand

And most importantly
Shine for yourself
Illuminate your own path
Don't wait for someone to do it for you
All that you will ever need
Is within you

Final Reflections

How do you feel about your ability to connect with your angel inside since completing this guide?

_____

_____

_____

_____

How do you now experience your angel inside as a result of the inspiration and guidance on these pages?

_____

_____

_____

_____

What guidance did you use in order to connect?

What went well? What challenges did you have?

Final Reflections

What changes have you made in your life since completing this guide?

_____

_____

_____

_____

_____

What benefits have you personally found from intentionally seeking connection with your angels?

_____

_____

_____

_____

_____

_____

The Angel Inside

Have you shared your experiences with anyone else? If so, what was the result?

_____

_____

_____

_____

_____

What have you learned about the role of your angel inside in your everyday life?

_____

_____

_____

_____

_____

Final Reflections

What additional tools do you need to feel even more connected to your angel inside? Where might you find what you need?

_____

_____

_____

_____

_____

_____

Acknowledgments

I wish to personally thank my family, friends, colleagues, teachers, and students for their contributions to my inspiration and knowledge and other support in creating this book:

- My publishing consultant, Sybil, for her unending patience with my indecision, procrastination, and perfectionism.

- My husband, Jake, for his unceasing support as I have chased all my chaotic whims, until I finally settled into my one true calling. I am eternally grateful for his love, encouragement, and insightful guidance.

- My children, London, Kallie, and Haley, who are the inspiration for all the work I do.

- My Cassiopeia: Emily, Carol, Julie, and Jennifer. For over 20 years, through happiness and heartache, these women have loved and supported me. Like their Greek goddess namesake, their inner beauty is unrivaled and their support in my life is irreplaceable.

- My sister, Meredith. Only she knows the secrets of our past; only she understands the indelible connection that binds us. Despite physical distance and busy lives, she is one of my biggest supporters.

- My friend, my student, my teacher, CaryAnne, who has been instrumental in supporting my growth and keeping me on the path.

- And finally, I am most grateful to one who is no longer with us, my mother, Ann Lisle Reed. Though she left us fourteen years ago at the time of this publication, her spirit has been felt in all that I have done during that time. It was her spirit that instilled in me the courage and the strength to finally pick up my pencil and allow the inspiration to flow through me onto the pages that would eventually become this book.

About The Author

Ashley Barnes, MS, is a poet, author, energist, coach, and Reiki Master/Teacher. She facilitates transformational experiences for soul-centered women who are waking up to their inner truth and feel guided to be of holistic service to the world. Most of these experiences come in the form of words; as a writer, her true love and gift is the written word. She also leads women's circles, workshops, and private sessions.

Ashley rediscovered her passion for writing nearly 15 years after losing her mother to a long battle with cancer, using poetry as an outlet for healing, exploration, and discovering her own deeper connection to her inner guidance. While *The Angel Inside* is her first printed work, Ashley also publishes articles and poems for various online magazines and blogs, such as *Elephant Journal, The Wellness Universe, and Sivana East*. She continues to write and regularly post poems, as well as the Daily Bliss, on her own blog.

In addition to writing, Ashley enjoys her 10+ year career in leadership and organizational development, where she gets to support individuals and organizations to grow holistically while also funding her creative work. She's happily married with four children, a granddaughter, and too many pets to list. She lives in "Kentuckiana" USA; however, her heart is always in the magical sand and glorious green water of Siesta Key Beach.

If you want to learn more about Ashley's work, read the Daily Bliss, and learn when her next book will come out, visit her website at http://www.aspiritledlife.org, where you can sign up to receive updates and inspiration.

If you enjoyed this book, I would really appreciate a review at Amazon.com as reviews are the life-blood of books.

You can also leave comment at my website: ASpiritLedLife.org/book

www.ingramcontent.com/pod-product-compliance
Lightning Source LLC
Chambersburg PA
CBHW032038290426
44110CB00012B/860